Original title:
Trunks of Truth

Copyright © 2025 Creative Arts Management OÜ
All rights reserved.

Author: Elliot Harrison
ISBN HARDBACK: 978-1-80567-412-2
ISBN PAPERBACK: 978-1-80567-711-6

The Canopy of Age-Old Secrets

Leaves whisper tales in the breeze,
Old branches giggle, if you please.
Gnarled knots hold laughter and lore,
Swaying softly, they beg for more.

Shaded patches hide little quirks,
Squirrels plot in their sneaky smirks.
With every creak, the old tree jokes,
It teases bees and tickles folks.

Enlightenment in the Twisted Bough

Up above, the branches bend,
Sharing giggles to no end.
Twisted paths where wisdom grows,
Who knew trees had such grand prose?

The owls hoot with sage disguise,
While wisecracks escape their eyes.
Here, the bark has quite the flair,
Banter that floats upon the air.

Roots of the Ancients

Down below, the roots entwine,
With little riddles, they align.
Beneath the soil, they twist and tease,
Holding secrets on the breeze.

Ancient tales drip from their tips,
As bugs giggle in their tight grips.
The ground shakes softly, what a sight,
As wisdom plays with day and night.

An Ode to the Inner Core

Hidden layers laugh at fate,
Spinning stories, oh so great!
In the heart, the humor flows,
Winking deeply, it knows what grows.

Inside the bark, a party brews,
Where shadows dance, and chaos ensues.
Life's a jest, within this shell,
An echo of a cheeky bell.

Secrets Beneath the Bark

In the forest, whispers creep,
Where the squirrels play, secrets keep.
A tree with knots, a funny sight,
Hiding giggles from day to night.

The raccoons plot, they gather 'round,
To share tall tales that know no bound.
Bark that's rough but full of cheer,
Hiding secrets that we hold dear.

The Veins of Understanding

Underneath the surface bright,
Veins of humor twist with delight.
Each ring tells jokes in silent tone,
A story shared, not meant alone.

Laughter flows like sap through wood,
In every crevice, mischief stood.
With every crack, a giggle found,
In the heart of the life around.

Unfolding Layers of Insight

Peeling back layers, oh so light,
Comes a chuckle, a playful bite.
Each slice reveals a funny tale,
Of dancing beetles and moose that sail.

Wise old owls hoot with glee,
Spreading laughter beneath the tree.
Unraveling wisdom, one giggle at a time,
Nature's humor, a joyful rhyme.

Echoes in the Heartwood

Echoes bounce through branches wide,
Where laughter and wisdom coincide.
Heartwood whispers secrets so sweet,
Of giggly ants in a busy fleet.

Tree trunks laugh as they sway and bend,
Sharing tidbits on every trend.
Nature's jesters, roots intertwined,
In every twist, a joke defined.

Forests of the Undisclosed

In the woods where secrets play,
Squirrels plot in a sneaky way.
Trees have gossip, topsy-turvy,
Telling tales that are quite fun and swervy.

Mushrooms dance, a funky crew,
Whispering jokes known to just a few.
Leaves are chuckling, branches bend,
In this forest, giggles never end.

Rabbits rave about their jazzy nights,
While the owls swoon in silly flights.
Every root and every bark,
Shares a laugh when it gets dark.

So take a stroll, dive into the cheer,
Where tree trunks clap as you draw near.
In the shade of jocular leaves,
Lies a world that never grieves.

The Hidden Voice of the Trees

Beneath the canopy, whispers glow,
The trees conspire, a comical show.
Bark on bark, they laugh and tease,
Sharing punchlines with the breeze.

A pine sneezes, a cedar coughs,
They joke about the squirrels' doffs.
Roots entwined with punchy puns,
Nature's comedy has just begun.

In the shade of ferns, laughter flows,
As echoes bounce where sunlight glows.
A woodpecker drums a beat so sweet,
Tickling laughter at every tree seat.

So listen closely, as you roam,
In every crack, there's a leafy poem.
The trees may stand so proud and tall,
But they know how to have a ball!

Shadows of Understanding

In the garden of secrets, where gossip grows,
Silly rabbits debate what nobody knows.
They whisper of wisdom hung high in the air,
Yet all that we hear is a tale of despair.

A squirrel chimes in with a nutty old plot,
Claiming the moon's just a shine on a pot.
While wise old owls nod from their seats in the trees,
They chuckle at humans who take life with ease.

Canopy of Concealed Wisdom

Beneath a green canopy, wise shadows play,
With secrets and stories that twirl and sway.
A parrot squawks loudly, truth wrapped in a joke,
All the while hiding the laughter it stoke.

A raccoon shares gossip, with glee in its eyes,
Proclaiming each branch holds the best of the lies.
As leaves rustle softly, the truth may just slip,
We gather the stories, and take a quick sip.

Branches of Belief

The branches extend with opinions so bright,
Each twist and each turn is a whimsical flight.
A badger suggests that belief is a game,
While raccoons argue 'twas always the same.

With laughter they climb, to the very top,
Where the chatter of wisdom never does stop.
An acorn drops down, and an argument starts,
As the wise share their stories of shared broken hearts.

Heartwood of Honesty

In the core of each tree lies a fib or a truth,
A woodpecker claims honesty comes from youth.
Yet squirrels debate if the wood's really pure,
While plotting their pranks, that's for sure, that's for sure!

With every knock-knock, a secret unfolds,
As the wise ones stake claims on the stories they've told.
They laugh at the fables, the twists that they weave,
In the heartwood of forests, mischief's reprieve.

Fables Cradled in Growth

In a forest where oddities thrive,
A squirrel tried to take a dive.
He leapt from a branch, bold and spry,
And landed with mud on his tie.

The trees giggled, their laughter loud,
As he stood up, oh so proud.
A frog croaked, 'What a noble feat!'
'Next time, try not to land on your feet!'

A wise owl hooted from a high trunk,
'Adventure is great, but that was just junk!'
The squirrel shrugged, brushed off the leaves,
'At least I amused all you mischief thieves!'

So fables were spun from that day forth,
About brave critters who ventured south.
Now every critter, big or small,
Knows that laughter is the best of all!

Twisted Paths of Discovery

One day a hedgehog took a stroll,
He stumbled upon a batty role.
He followed a path all bent and twisted,
With every wrong turn, he felt so misfit.

A snail said, 'This was not planned!'
As they both peered at a map, oh so grand.
'Very useful, but upside down,' squeaked the snail,
'No wonder we keep hitting the trail!'

A wise fox chuckled as he passed by,
'You two will surely reach the sky!'
But getting lost was part of the fun,
Amid the laughter under the sun.

So, when they finally reached their goal,
They found more joy than a simple stroll.
'Let's do it again!' the hedgehog did shout,
For wandering aimlessly leads to a route.

Heart of the Forest's Secrets

Deep in the woods, where giggles blend,
A bear tried to dance, who knew, my friend!
He stumbled and tripped on his big furry feet,
While the rabbits all chirped, 'Is this a retreat?'

With branches a-swaying beneath the sun,
The bear took a bow and said, 'Aren't we fun?'
But the trees were shocked, they'd never seen,
A bear doing ballet with such a keen!

The deer cheered loud, 'You've stolen the show!'
While others all wondered, 'Where did he go?'
He twirled and he jumped without a care,
The heart of the forest drew him to share.

In the end, it was clear and bright,
Everyone danced under the stars of night.
Secrets emerge in laughter and claps,
As nature reveals its fun-loving maps!

Whispers Among the Canopy

Underneath branches where secrets are spun,
A woodpecker knocked like he was having fun.
He tapped on a tree with a rhythmic beat,
While ants formed a band at his tiny feet.

The wind whispered tales of a goofball night,
Where critters all gathered, hearts full of light.
A badger in shades played the saxophone,
While a hedgehog stomped with a groan and a moan.

Laughter echoed through the leafy embrace,
As each animal tried to keep up the pace.
A parrot squawked, 'No, don't stop the tunes!'
While raccoons danced under the watchful moons.

So if you wander where whispers flow,
Remember the critters, putting on a show.
Among the branches and laughter bright,
Is where funny fables take flight each night!

Fragmented Foundations

In a world of mismatched socks,
Lies the truth that really rocks.
Foundations made of sandwich bread,
Where all the wobbly dreams are fed.

Cats in bow ties, dogs on skateboards,
Building castles with plastic swords.
Revealed secrets through playful games,
The hidden truths wear silly names.

Laughter echoes in the void,
Where honesty gets overjoyed.
Each crumb of truth a tasty treat,
Disguised in candy for all to eat.

The Unraveling Canopy

Beneath the trees, a squirrel's prank,
Brings truth to life with a nutty clank.
Branches waving like silly hats,
Whispers of wisdom from giggling rats.

A leaf reveals a secret song,
The truth can play with what's gone wrong.
When nature plays on a rubber band,
It stretches laughs across the land.

In this wild and twisted space,
Every truth wears a funny face.
With twigs as microphones in tow,
It's clear that honesty likes to show!

Patterns of Perception

With polka dots upon my shirt,
I dance through life without a hurt.
Perceptions swirl like paint on walls,
Truth twists as easily as falls.

In funny hats, we wear our pride,
Finding jest in what we hide.
A tuba's honk or accordion's squeeze,
Turns wisdom into fits of wheeze.

Patterns shift like jello's jig,
Shaping truths that seem so big.
In every joke, there's wisdom spun,
Yet giggles drown the serious fun.

Hideaways of Humanity

In cozy nooks where secrets play,
Humans hide their truth each day.
Behind the couch or under beds,
Lies laughter softly filling heads.

A clown car parked in the living room,
Brings hidden truths that start to bloom.
Peeking out from silly places,
Life unfolds in laughing faces.

In every shadow, stories dwell,
Funny truths that weave and swell.
With every giggle shared in cheer,
Humanity's heart becomes quite clear.

The Stand of Forgotten Truths

In a forest of odd claims,
The trees start to shake with fame.
One swears it can fly with ease,
While another argues over bees.

Leaves whisper secrets so absurd,
Like gossip echoing from a bird.
A squirrel grins, with nuts in hand,
Claiming he's the wisest in the land.

Mushrooms chuckle, sprouting tall,
Saying they've seen it all, after all.
"Who needs a book for all that lore?
Just ask the roots, they know much more!"

And when the wind starts to narrate,
The trees all lean in, despite fate.
Each twist and turn a silly hoot,
In this wood, fact wears a funny suit.

Timbered Dialogues and Echoes

In the shade where whispers roam,
Bark and leaves create a home.
One log claims it saw the moon,
While another laughed, "That's just a tune!"

Branches stretch like arms out wide,
"Can you truly trust the tide?"
They debate the squirrels' silly tales,
While wind joins in, flapping sails.

"Why do pinecones keep their cool?
Because they're totally the rule!"
The oak just nods, with eyes so bright,
"They think they're stars, from day to night."

With every laugh, a new truth sprouts,
In this grove, skepticism shouts.
Tall tales twisted in bark's embrace,
In timbered echoes, we find our place.

Underneath the Mossy Truth

Beneath the leaves, the comedy awaits,
Moss plays tricks on old, bent crates.
"Did I really just see a frog?"
"Or was it just my old dog's smog?"

The ferns giggle, swaying with glee,
"Stop asking me, just let it be!"
A beetle rolls a ball of sass,
Claiming it's the life of the grass.

"Why grow up when I can hide?
I know more than I can ever provide!"
Roots curl up, in laughter they shake,
As shadows dance beside the lake.

A whisper passes, playful and sly,
"Every truth deserves a try!"
Underneath where humor blooms,
The forest breathes in delightful fumes.

Narratives Shrouded in Green

In a glen where the stories twist,
Greenery giggles as they persist.
An ivy vine spins tales that rise,
"Last week, I saw gnomes wearing ties!"

A willow swings, with branches low,
"Let's not forget the dancing crow!"
They plot and plan their nightly spree,
While butterflies join as light company.

"Remember that time we snuck a peek?
Mice thought they'd found a hidden creek!"
The laughter swells like a bubbling brook,
As roots wrap around the joyful nook.

With every leaf that flutters down,
A new narrative wears a crown.
In this green world, where smiles entwine,
Every punchline's a twist in the pine.

The Silent Exchange of Leaves

In a whispering breeze, they meet,
A dance of green with tiny feet.
Leaves gossip soft of growing old,
Secrets in rustles, stories told.

Each cycle spins a fresh debate,
Who is wise and who is straight?
The oak rolls eyes at the young sprout,
"You're growing fast, but what's that about?"

They chuckle loud when storms take flight,
A leaf in denial, "It's just a slight!"
Yet when the sun paints colors bright,
They marvel at the day and night.

In the autumn, hues they flaunt,
Pretending age, but they just vaunt.
A timeless jest amid the sway,
In laughter's shade, they wish to stay.

The Dialogues of Decay

Amid the cracks and crumbling bark,
Old tree meets squirrel with a spark.
"What's that smell?" asks the weary branch,
"Just old age, buddy, trying to dance!"

The squirrel laughs, "You still look spry,
In your leafy suit, oh me, oh my!"
The tree replies with a hearty creak,
"Gravity isn't just for the meek!"

In shadows cast by bending light,
They joke of blooms in spring's first sight.
"Remember when you climbed so high?
I fell and laughed, oh my, oh my!"

When winter's chill starts to grow,
They share tales of seeds they know.
With each falling flake and sigh of breeze,
They find their joy in playful tease.

Hidden Histories in the Wood

Deep in the woods where whispers dwell,
A log recounts all things that fell,
"How'd you get those lines of age?"
"Cut to the chase, don't turn the page!"

Behind every knot, a story lies,
Of critters, storms, and starlit skies.
"Isn't that chip from the old axe?"
"Ah, yes, but it's just part of the facts!"

The fungi giggle, sharing lore,
"Did you see the owl that swore?
He's wise, yet forgets where he's perched,
A tale worth telling, well-researched!"

As rustling leaves join the chatter,
They debate on what really matters.
In silence, they laugh, a woodsy crew,
With jokes of the past still feeling new.

Saplings and Secrets

Little saplings stretch towards the sun,
"Can't wait to grow, it'll be such fun!"
The elder says with a knowing nod,
"Patience, dear one, don't be a fraud!"

With tiny leaves, they play and sway,
"The wind is cool, let's shout hooray!"
The roots beneath, they twist and talk,
"Don't take life too seriously, just walk!"

Each bud compares its growth with pride,
"I'll be so tall, I'll touch the sky!"
"Maybe, but must avoid that fence,"
"Sure! But fences are just past tense!"

In the shade, they scheme and dream,
With visions grand of a leafy team.
From tiny seeds, laughter will spring,
As secrets turn into flowering.

Roots of Revelation

In a garden dense with fibrous cheer,
Wiggly worms trade gossip so dear.
Discoveries sprout where secrets are sown,
A mustached mole claims he found a new bone.

The daisies giggle as sunshine knocks,
While rabbits debate in mismatched socks.
Truth hides beneath unpruned hedges,
Where plants weave tales of hedgehog pledges.

Ninjas of nature, they dance through the dew,
Tickling each leaf and shaking them too.
A beetle boasts of a race with a snail,
While butterflies argue who's fresher in pale.

Laughter erupts from within the sweet roots,
As the cabbage confides in the jellybeans' boots.
The turnips grumble, but can't make a scene,
With humor in harvests they surely glean.

Veins of Veracity

Beneath the surface, the laughter flows,
Like rivers of truth in a world full of prose.
The carrots insult each other's size,
While squashes reveal their surprising disguise.

A broccoli fluffs its odd green crown,
Pretending to wear the most regal gown.
"Who knew veggies could spin such a tale?"
As garlic concedes, "I once didn't smell stale!"

Fungi giggle in their caps and gowns,
As beans tell stories of faraway towns.
A potato dreams of being a chef,
Whipping up dishes that leave a good rep!

The cabbage declares a bizarre fest,
With radishes sharing their wittiest jest.
And in every vein, secrets bubble and churn,
In the garden of laughter, there's so much to learn!

Whispering Woods

In a forest where mushy stories bloom,
And squirrels wear hats, dispelling all gloom.
Trees share their tales with roots held so tight,
A wise old oak speaks of a moonlit fright.

The ferns giggle as they sway in the breeze,
While crickets chime with the greatest of ease.
"Did you hear?" chirp the robins so bold,
"We're planning a party, with snacks to behold!"

With daisies as dancers, they twirl and twist,
A woodpecker joins in, how could he resist?
Each whisper a riddle, a chuckle, a cheer,
In the woods where laughter is always near.

The mushrooms concoct some odd fruity brew,
While owls hoot jokes, "Hoo needs a new view?"
And as day turns to night, the giggling persists,
In this magical place where the fun never quits.

Echoes of Existence

In the depths where echoes softly play,
A chorus of banter brightens the day.
"Who's the funniest critter?" they all gasp and jest,
As shadows dance wildly and hearts feel blessed.

The chipmunks' chatter rings clear and loud,
While foxes prance proudly, heads in a cloud.
"A fox without greed is a rare sight indeed!"
Laughter erupts; it's all they need.

Through valleys and hills where giggles resound,
Every creature here wears joy like a crown.
The hedgehogs roll in the grassy terrain,
With snippets of whimsy making their gain.

As echoes bounce back with whimsical cheer,
They tell of the moments we all hold dear.
In a world where truth wears a humorous coat,
Life's too short; let's all learn to gloat!

Barked Confessions

In the forest, secrets sway,
Trees gossip in their own way.
A squirrel steals, a bird just sings,
Wooden tales of unlikely things.

The old oak chuckles, holds a jest,
While the pine stands tall, over the rest.
With leaves aflutter, stories are spun,
Nature's laughter, oh what fun!

Roots entangle with tales untold,
Whispering mischief, brave and bold.
Raccoons dance like they own the night,
Each trunk knows the punchline just right.

So when you stroll on a sunny trail,
Listen close, heed the woodsy tale.
For nature's voices, in rustles and creaks,
Share humor that brightens our heaviest weeks.

Nature's Unseen Chronicles

Beneath the bark, a world is hum,
Where caterpillars strut and drums go thrum.
The bushes gossip, the flowers giggle,
As ants march by, in a tiny wiggle.

A beetle boasts of his shiny shell,
While crickets chirp of the dance they fell.
Butterflies flutter, showing off flair,
Nature's journal is everywhere!

Rabbits nibble on the grass so green,
While talking trees swap stories unseen.
Each rustling leaf sings a little tune,
Mischief managed under the moon.

If only trees could share their lore,
We'd all learn to laugh, and so much more!
In the woodland realm, humor rarely fades,
With every branch, an anecdote cascades.

The Archive of Ancient Wisdom

Beneath every knot, a story hides,
Whispers of laughter where wisdom abides.
Old stumps know secrets from days of yore,
While mushrooms giggle on the forest floor.

Birch trees jive with their odorous bark,
Sharing tales that make a dull day spark.
The owl hoots twice, nudging the fox,
As they recount the time of the landed socks!

Here in the woods, laughter rings clear,
With each passing moment, the tales appear.
Nature's wise ones, in shadows they dwell,
Witty little nuggets only time will tell.

So sit on a log, lend an ear to the breeze,
And gather the humor that flows with such ease.
For every cinch and every twist,
Nature's archive is hard to resist!

Branching Out in Awareness

From each branch, new stories sprout,
In the canopy, laughter's about.
With leaves a-dancing in gentle cheer,
Nature's quirks bring a smile, never a fear.

The groundhog grins from his cozy hole,
As squirrels practice their quest for a pole.
The wind tells jokes with a playful shove,
While blossoms bloom, and friendships shove.

Lizards bask in sunny spots,
While ants throw parties, living in knots.
Breezes play tag, rustling through trees,
In this merry place, life's a breeze!

Embrace the weird, and reach for the sun,
Branch out in joy, there's plenty for fun.
For in this garden where laughter grows,
Awareness blooms, and happiness flows.

Tales of the Forgotten Grove

In the grove where whispers sing,
Squirrels wear capes, doing their thing.
They chat about the nutty stew,
Gossiping 'bout the things they knew.

A raccoon stole a pie one night,
Left the chef in quite a fright.
The owls hooted with delight,
Wishing they had taken a bite.

Trees play poker with the sun,
Moonbeam dealers having fun.
Roots laugh, tangled in their game,
While branches shout, "I'm not to blame!"

Beneath the leaves, the secrets flow,
Tales that only critters know.
So if you dare, just come and see,
The wild antics of a tree-celebrity!

Acorns of Hidden Knowledge

Acorns roll with clever plans,
Whispering in their tiny cans.
They plot how to outsmart the cat,
While wearing tiny hats—imagine that!

A wise old oak begins to snore,
While chipmunks dance and beg for more.
They shuffle through the leafy lore,
Taking bets on who'll win the score.

A dance-off breaks out by the creek,
Nutty grooves make everyone squeak.
The shyest tree joins in the fray,
And even the moss starts to sway!

In every crack and cranny wide,
Jokes of nature cannot hide.
So gather round, both wild and tame,
For acorns tell the funniest tales, not the same!

The Buried Seeds of Truth

Seeds are buried, secrets low,
Digging deep, but what do they know?
A worm chuckles, wriggles with glee,
As plants wonder where they'll be.

The sunflower spreads gossip tall,
Claiming it saw the toadstool fall.
"I swear I heard a tree joke, too!"
But the trees just chuckle, "What's new?"

A little fern, sharp as a tack,
Whispers tales behind the back.
"They're planting stories, so absurd,
And none can trust an old, wise bird."

So when you walk, remember this rhyme,
Seeds and stories have their time.
Beneath the soil, laughter grows,
With tales that tickle—all that you know!

Whispers of the Arbor

The arboreal crowd gathers around,
With roots intertwined beneath the ground.
Whispers fly from leaf to leaf,
Tales of mischief causing grief.

A squirrel stole a hat from a man,
Who stormed about, turned beet-red and tan.
The boughs shook with hearty laughter,
As nature planned its next big chapter.

A raccoon got caught in a jam,
With sticky paws and a green ham.
"We'll tell the world this silly blunder,"
The trees echoed, shaking in thunder!

So join the chorus of giggling trees,
In the park, where laughter's a breeze.
For every whisper, a joke to share,
With roots and branches, it's always fair!

Beneath the Surface of Solitude

In the forest, where whispers dwell,
A squirrel claims a nutty shell.
His acorn stash, a treasure trove,
Where secrets lie, and jesters rove.

Each leaf a giggle, each branch a laugh,
Nature's humor in every half.
A twig might trip, a root might tease,
In solitude, find joy with ease.

Raccoons wear masks with style and flair,
Stealing snacks without a care.
In a world where silence reigns,
Laughter echoes through the plains.

So if you wander, take a peek,
At nature's jokes, so sly, so chic.
Beneath the stillness, life's a play,
In the woods, fun finds its way.

The Lore Behind Each Ring

Count the rings, a wise old tree,
Each one tells tales, quite funny, you see.
A love story, a bird's nest gone wrong,
Secrets hidden in nature's old song.

One year, a goat made quite the fuss,
Climbing high, giving the tree a thrust.
Each bark gnarled with laughter's trace,
Nature's diary, a jocular space.

A woodpecker with rhythm and flair,
Tapping beats, a woodland affair.
Making music with a beak so fine,
A concert in branches, simply divine.

So gather round, hear tales unfold,
Each ring a giggle, each story bold.
In the cedar's heart, humor rings true,
A woodland lore for me and you.

Revelation Rooted in Nature

In the dirt, where earthworms wriggle,
Come find the truth with a jolly giggle.
Each root a riddle, each sprout a jest,
Nature's wisdom, oddly blessed.

The daisies dance, quite unaware,
Of serious matters, they don't care.
With petals bright and sunshine gay,
They laugh at clouds, come what may.

A thunderstorm with a booming sound,
Leaves everyone soaking on the ground.
Yet rainbows rise, with colors bright,
Turning puddles to pure delight.

So stroll the fields, lose all your woes,
Nature's joke shop, where laughter grows.
In every bloom, find smiles unchained,
In the heart of the earth, joy is ingrained.

Secrets Within the Boughs

Beneath the branches, secrets play,
With a gossipy owl who won't delay.
"Did you hear about the frisky hare?"
"Word spreads fast, so lend me your ear."

A raccoon with a penchant for cheese,
Sneaks a snack with utmost ease.
While chipmunks squabble, in a comic fight,
Over acorns and laughter, their favorite delight.

Each bough a stage, each leaf a fan,
Nature's circus, without a plan.
A fox in socks, with a fancy strut,
Will steal your heart and a tasty nut.

So next time you wander, take in the sounds,
Nature holds secrets in playful bounds.
In every rustle, a chuckle awaits,
Under the boughs, where humor creates.

The Soul's Silhouette

Hidden tales in shadows creep,
Whispers shared, secrets to keep.
A penguin dons a silly hat,
Dances like a clumsy cat.

Laughter echoes in the night,
As the stars join in the flight.
The moon winks with cheeky glee,
While trees chuckle silently.

A squirrel juggles acorn snacks,
Chasing dreams on little tracks.
Daring leaps, a playful spry,
A swingless swing, oh me, oh my!

In this realm of silly schemes,
Where nonsense joins the wild dreams.
The silhouette of joy we trace,
In shadows where we find our place.

Unseen Boundaries

The fence that bends with every breeze,
Invites the cats to climb with ease.
They tumble over, bold and spry,
Delighting in the curious sky.

Invisible lines that seldom show,
Split gardens where the daisies grow.
But bees just buzz and giggle loud,
As they flit past this lazy crowd.

The dog next door, a daring chap,
Wants to play a game of tap.
He bounds beneath the welcome sign,
With shenanigans that feel divine.

Boundaries blur in every laugh,
Where mischief's peace is the best half.
Cats and dogs unite for fun,
In a world where rules are none!

Nature's Narrative

In a meadow filled with cheer,
Woodpeckers peck, we stop to hear.
A story spun by nature's hand,
Where laughter rustles through the land.

The grass decides to tickle toes,
As flowers peek and giggle shows.
A butterfly in disco strut,
Wings aflutter, shaking butt.

Turtles race without a care,
While frogs leap forth, a daring glare.
Nature's tale is never tame,
With comedy, it plays its game!

The creek chuckles as it flows,
With silly rocks and slippery toes.
In this lively, laughing dance,
Life interprets joy at every chance.

The Hidden Harvest

In the garden, veggies roam,
Tomatoes stealing broccoli's home.
Carrots giggle, green tops tease,
While radishes hide in leafy freeze.

The pumpkin's prance, a jolly sight,
Winking at the stars so bright.
Eggplants pirouette with flair,
In a world that simply doesn't care.

Peas meet beans in a goofy chat,
Raccoons plan a veggie spat.
The harvest smiles, a bountiful show,
As critters join the garden glow.

From hidden patches, joy spills forth,
Nature's antics, what a worth!
In laughter's shade, we gather round,
For in this plot, true fun is found.

The Hidden Canopy of Clarity

Underneath the leafy shade,
Secrets hide, but some invade.
Squirrels gossip, branches sway,
In this world, they come to play.

Whispers float on gentle breeze,
Revelations come with ease.
A rabbit laughs at what they tell,
Life's a joke, we're all under a spell.

Mushrooms smile with curious sighs,
Their little caps are all the wise.
With every flick of furry tail,
A riddle pops, a silly tale.

When rains come down, the joy reveals,
Life's a dance on muddy wheels.
Each drop's a jester, glinting bright,
In this canopy of silly light.

Sheltered Stories in the Wilderness

In a nook where shadows play,
Frogs recite their rhymed ballet.
Every croak, a history,
A leap into the mystery.

Trees chuckle with rustling leaves,
Tales of little mischief thieves.
Nuts and berries, the banquet spread,
Squirrels scheme of plunder ahead.

Under each root, a laugh survives,
Where critters plot their little jives.
Hares hop lightly, sharing cheer,
"What's so funny?" you might hear.

Amid the bramble, wisdom lies,
Wrapped in humor, oh so sly.
Take a seat, enjoy the show,
In the wild, the laughs just flow.

The Map of Life's Lessons

On paper made from woven vines,
The path of life, where humor shines.
With arrows drawn by birds above,
Every bend's a twist of love.

Follow where the raccoons tread,
With giggles bubbling up instead.
Each landmark hides a funny quirk,
Where even shadows seem to smirk.

A map in hand, we waddle on,
Through puddles deep, till shoes are gone.
Compass spins, but hearts stay true,
Where laughter guides us, we break through.

Each step a dance, with joy we choose,
In every stumble, we can't refuse.
Follow the laughs, be brave and bold,
Our story's worth more than gold.

Wisdom Dripping from Leaves

In the morning light, they greet the day,
Droplets sparkle, come out to play.
Each leaf holds tales from storms and sun,
Sipping wisdom, just for fun.

Breezes tickle the branches wide,
As squirrels gather, all filled with pride.
Fables drip from boughs of green,
In every giggle, there's more to glean.

As we sip life's curious brew,
Nature whispers secrets true.
With every chuckle, we bloom and grow,
In laughter's arms, we find our flow.

A forest filled with merry signs,
Life's lessons wrapped in playful lines.
So raise a toast to skies above,
For wisdom drips in waves of love.

Harvesting the Unuttered

In the orchard of silent screams,
Apples hang in golden beams.
With whispers caught in fruity skins,
We gather laughs; let the fun begin!

Underneath a sunlit sky,
The cheeky pears laugh as they lie.
Plucking joy from leafy boughs,
Silly truths, here are your vows!

Cherries giggle, plums roll away,
With jokes they toss into the fray.
Laughter ripens; we reap the cheer,
Harvesting whispers, never fear!

Here's to the fruits that cheekily cling,
To untold tales that make us sing.
In this garden of jest and fun,
We've proven truth can weigh a ton!

The Gnarled Tale

From wooden knots, a story drips,
Of cheeky squirrels and sliding slips.
Beneath the bark, a giggle hides,
In twisted limbs where humor bides.

Roots entwined in laughter, winks,
Conspiracies whisper in the kinks.
A gnarled branch up high does sway,
While trunks of mirth make fun at play.

The whispers of this knotted plight,
Bring comedic sparks and sheer delight.
In every curl a jest resides,
As nature's giggles dully chides.

So heed the boughs, their tales unwind,
In twisted woods, true wit you'll find.
With laughter caught in knots and bends,
Let every gnarled tale make amends.

Beneath Layers of Existence

Beneath the skin of earthy earth,
Lurks wisdom wrapped in playful mirth.
Each layer holds a chuckle deep,
Where silly secrets slyly creep.

As roots exchange well-timed quips,
And dirt delights in cheeky flips.
What lies below is pure surprise,
While laughter sprout, no need for lies.

In every twist, a laugh resides,
Like tiny sprites in rooty slides.
They dance and tickle with delight,
In layers thick, we find the light.

So dig below, and you may see,
That fun and truth are harmony.
With every scoop, a chuckle loud,
Unearth the joy, make nature proud!

The Silent Arbor of Revelation

In an arbor where secrets sway,
Silent whispers lead the way.
Branches point with knowing glee,
As laughter blooms from each decree.

A bird who speaks in silent code,
Sings of fun while chewing 'toad'.
Leaves tickle cheeks in breezy strolls,
With punchlines waiting in the shoals.

Gnarled roots of humor stretch and clasp,
In ancient knots, we dare to grasp.
Revelations twirl in shadowed light,
Tickling thought until insight.

So stroll beneath this leafy dome,
Where every truth feels like a home.
In quietude, let laughter reign,
In the silent grove, joy is the gain!

The Understory of Existence

In the forest where whispers play,
Tales of mischief frolic each day.
Mice wear capes, squirrels on chairs,
Plotting to steal the humans' pears.

With roots that twist like gossip's thread,
Every shadow has secrets, it's said.
Beneath the canopy, laughter's heard,
While critters debate who saw the bird.

A frog wearing glasses reads from a book,
While ants in a line keep a watchful look.
The raccoons conspire to steal a goldfish,
In this leafy realm, they live and they wish.

So among the plants, the jokes take flight,
In the greenhooded laughter, day turns to night.
Existence is silly, yet deeply profound,
In the layers of life, the humor is found.

Leaves of Unspoken Truths

The leaves are gossiping, swaying with glee,
Whispering tales of the creatures they see.
A worm in a bowtie, quite dapper indeed,
Claims he knows secrets, but what does he need?

The wind laughs aloud as it twirls in delight,
Spinning the stories that dance in the light.
Each rustle a chuckle, each flutter a grin,
While beetles debate who will start the spin.

The flowers are nodding, they join in the fun,
As buds burst with humor beneath the warm sun.
Bumblebees jest about stings and such,
In the garden of laughter, they chatter so much.

So take a moment, lean in, hear them share,
The wisdom of leaves caught up in the air.
With each little chuckle, a truth must emerge,
Life's funny little secrets in giggles converge.

Memory Knotting in the Timber

Round and round, the branches sway,
Knotting memories in a playful display.
A woodpecker's joke rings out with a tap,
While squirrels share stories under the map.

Time may tie knots, but laughter unspools,
Revealing the lightness of life's little duels.
A beaver is building a slapstick dam,
Where gags and puns snicker and jam.

Old logs roll back with a creak and a sigh,
Telling tall tales as the winds flutter by.
Every twist and turn, a chuckle, a jest,
In the timbered halls, humor's a guest.

The memories spin 'round like vines in a race,
Entwined in the laughter, they find their own place.
In this forest of mirth, snapshots reveal,
The joy tied in knots, oh what a big deal!

Rings of Perception

Count the rings on the old tree's face,
Each one a laugh at life's quick-paced race.
A raccoon once claimed he was older than time,
But age is just number, not a person's prime.

With each layer added, stories unfold,
Of squirrels in suits and robins so bold.
They mock the wise owl, adjusting his specs,
In a tree full of jesters, all hoping for checks.

The leaves chuckle softly, the bark rolls its eyes,
As each ring holds the lore of the skies.
With memories made, some silly and bright,
They dance in the breeze, a comical sight.

So come take a gander at nature's great joke,
In the rings of perception, truth's veil we poke.
Laughter's the heartbeat of everyone here,
In this forest, the fun is quite clear!

Overgrown Paths of Insight

In a forest where logic got quite lost,
Trees debate, never counting the cost.
One says, 'I'm taller, I've seen it all!'
Another cracks up, 'You're just here to brawl!'

Branches gossip in the humorous breeze,
Shaking their leaves with such wondrous ease.
'What's the matter with the squirrels?' they jest,
'Why do they think they're the absolute best?'

Pinecones roll down, full of bravado,
Claiming their wisdom, ranging from near to far.
"Listen close, nature's the perfect teacher!"
And all the bushes just laugh, "What a preacher!"

But as nature chuckles, it's hard to resolve,
What's learned in the woods that no one can solve.
Logs keep it secret, laughing in tone,
Nature's a goofball, never alone!

The Heartwood's Soliloquy

In the core of the tree, a tale does unfold,
Of soft heartwood laughing, quite bold and uncontrolled.
'Why do humans pine for leaves in the air?'
'When roots tell the jokes from their underground chair!'

Sap drips like coffee, oh what a brew,
Don't spill the truth, or it might squirt too.
'What makes a tree stump roll on the floor?'
'Simply the laughter, forever to soar!'

Knots twist with humor, tangled and bright,
Their backstories colored in shades of delight.
'Not every ring tells of years, that's a myth!'
'Some simply narrate a funny old skit!'

So, hark to the laughter of heartwood so wise,
It whispers the secrets beneath vast skies.
'If you're seeking the truth, take a seat and enjoy!
For the sound of the wood is the world's greatest toy!'

Shadows of the Old Sentinel

Beneath the great oak, shadows play tricks,
Whispering stories of cheeky old stints.
'What did the branch say to the wind on a dare?'
'I'm too grounded for drama, don't you give me a scare!'

Squirrels plot mischief, creating a scene,
While shadows agree, 'It's all quite serene!'
'Why do you climb, little critters so spry?'
'It's all for the nuts, and a view of the sky!'

Leaves rustle, joining in on the jest,
'Who'd thought that shade could be such a pest?'
The boughs crack up, a wise elder's delight,
'Join us in laughter; it's a beautiful sight!'

The old sentinel chuckles from ages before,
Entwined in the laughter that roots can restore.
With humor as armor, they weather each storm,
The shadows keep dancing, their spirits so warm!

Recollections from the Canopy

Oh, to swing in the treetops, a dance in the sun,
Birds chirp in laughter, oh, aren't they fun?
'Did you see that owl, with its serious face?'
'It thinks it's a sage, but it's lost in space!'

The leaves start to quiver, a chuckling refrain,
Each memory tells tales of delightful disdain.
'What speaks to the clouds when they rumble away?'
'It's just the trees laughing; that's how we play!'

So much to ponder up high in the green,
Where whispers of wisdom strut bold and serene.
'Tell me a secret, oh mighty pine tree!'
'Why yes, they all giggle, just wait and you'll see!'

For up in the canopy, joy takes its flight,
Where laughter is plenty, and visions are bright.
Recollections rain down, a wonderful show,
With humor as harvest, and joy as it grows!

The Inner Grove

In the grove where secrets grow,
Trees wear hats of mistletoe.
Squirrels gossip, nuts in tow,
What they'll do, we'll never know.

The owls hoot with splendid flair,
Critiquing leaves, without a care.
A raccoon dances, what a pair,
Chasing shadows in the air.

Each twig a story, tall and proud,
Twirling tales to any crowd.
Laughter bounces, nice and loud,
In this grove, we're quite allowed.

So let's sip on dew, take a seat,
Behind a trunk, it's quite a treat.
Join the party, feel the beat,
Nature's mischief can't be beat.

Forgotten Forks

In the drawer where chaos reigns,
Spoons and forks all have their claims.
Lost a knife? It's all the same,
Their laughter echoes, such silly games.

A fork insists it's quite the star,
"Look at me, I'm in a memoir!"
While spoons are dreaming of a car,
All in vain, they don't get far.

Yet each bite leads to more fun,
Spilling stories 'til we're done.
In this banquet, we all run,
Chasing crumbs beneath the sun.

So next time you set your table,
Remember forks, if you are able.
They're not just tools, they're quite stable,
Making meals a laughable fable.

Beneath the Surface

Down below the silver waves,
Fish swap jokes among the caves.
A crab with sass, oh, how he braves,
While jellyfish float in glowing raves.

The seahorse spins a tale so wild,
Of lost flip-flops, cheerfully piled.
Every barnacle, a treasure filed,
In this world, where joy is styled.

A turtle grins, "I know a joke!"
While seaweed dances like it's woke.
Each bubble bursts with laughter's cloak,
Making waves, the ocean's yoke.

So let's dive deep, forget the shore,
Underwater giggles we adore.
In this realm, forevermore,
Let's splash and snicker, never bore.

The Weight of Whispers

In quiet corners, where secrets dwell,
Whispers giggle like a mischievous spell.
A breeze carries tales, oh, what a swell,
Each one a laugh, casting a shell.

"Did you hear about the snail?" one sighs,
Who dreamed of soaring up to the skies.
His shell was heavy with all his ties,
But he cracked a joke, and we all rise.

The shadows chuckle, fluttering near,
As stories dance on edges clear.
Beneath the stars, we shed our fear,
And every giggle, we hold dear.

So gather close, in twilight's glow,
Each soft murmur, let it flow.
In the weight of whispers, we still glow,
With laughter trails, forever in tow.

Tender Bark

Beneath the layers, soft and shy,
Secrets rustle, oh my oh my!
Squirrels giggle, as they conspire,
To unearth tales that spark desire.

Branches wave in playful glee,
Tickling the winds, wild and free.
While birds plot their next big heist,
A nutty feast, oh what a feast!

Tough Stories

Here lies a tale, old as the hills,
Of acorns lost and silly spills.
The wise old owl rolls his eyes,
At the gossip shared 'neath bright blue skies.

Bark tells of storms, and sunny days,
Of rabbits who danced in hilarious ways.
Tripping wildly in moonlit drawers,
We laugh at life, that rugged chore!

The Shelter of Sheltered Realities

Within the shadows of bark-tipped dreams,
Chaos hides, laughing in streams.
Where sunlight shimmers with a wink,
And all the critters pause to think.

A fox in slippers, a raccoon in bows,
Belly laughs bursting, as mischief grows.
Caterpillars boast of fashion goals,
In this refuge where humor rolls!

Leaves that Hold Sagas

Oh, listen close to the leaves that sway,
Whispering secrets of yesterday.
A dance of green with funny tunes,
Tickling the air under cheeky moons.

Each rustle a giggle, a narrative spun,
Of clumsy beetles and races run.
The tales do twist, and turn with flair,
In this zany world, we all share!

Grove of the Unrevealed

Gather 'round in the grove of jest,
Where laughter hides and mischief rests.
Trees gossip in a language sly,
While shadows chuckle and spirits fly.

Beneath the canopy, secrets unfold,
Jokes of the ancients, delightfully bold.
In this wood, all we need is cheer,
For every chuckle brings us near!

Telling Trees of the Hidden

Innocent whispers, leaves that chuckle,
Frogs on branches, oh what a shuffle,
Squirrels gossip in acorn hats,
Sharing secrets with the silly cats.

Hidden jokes in bark creases,
Tickling winds as laughter increases,
Branches wave like hands of cheer,
Nature's jesters, always near.

The trunks stand tall with wisdom sly,
Yet bark beetles buzz by with a sigh,
They know the tales of critters bold,
Of nuts lost and mischief retold.

So when you pass those leafy giants,
Stick around for their comic science,
For each old tree spins a yarn,
Making daylight feel less darn.

The Chronicle of the Aged Wood

Once there lived a wise old log,
Holding secrets like a sly green frog,
His limbs would creak with stories bright,
Of dancing squirrels in the moonlight.

Worms wiggled, thinking they were cool,
Performing stunts while others drool,
Beetles played on his wooden stage,
Creating laughter instead of rage.

The knots held fables of missed ties,
Of why leaves fall and why birds fly,
Echoing giggles in the summer light,
Woodland ballet, a comical sight.

With every ring, a joke old born,
In the midst of the forest, where no one's worn,
The aged wood chuckles through the years,
Spreading humor, dissolving fears.

Echoes in the Woodland Veil

Among the trees where laughter rings,
Pigeons punch lines with flapping wings,
Crickets chirp a funny rhyme,
While shadows dance in joyful mime.

Bushes hide giggles and wisecracks,
Tickling the path of the rambunctious tracks,
In the canopy, a parrot does squawk,
Reciting jokes as the squirrels gawk.

Mice in capes perform by the brook,
With antics more thrilling than a book,
Each rustle in the leaves has flair,
A laugh fest beneath the sun's glare.

So listen close, in this woody domain,
Where pranksters thrive, and sun drops rain,
The echoes of fun will never grow old,
In the woodland veil, laughter unfolds.

The Rooted Epiphany

Down beneath the earthy realm,
Witty roots set the tone at the helm,
With jokes whispered in soil below,
Cracking up the trees to and fro.

An old stump played a song so sweet,
Rabbits tapped their paws to the beat,
The grumpy thorns would chuckle in spite,
As flowers bloomed with peculiar delight.

One wise root said with a grin,
"Life's just a patch of wild spin!"
The tiny creatures gathered around,
Guffawing loudly, not a sad sound.

So next time you tread on grassy ground,
Remember the laughs that ever astound,
For beneath your feet, a party awaits,
With glee and giggles in nature's crates.

Growth and Grit

In the garden of dreams, we often fall,
Tripping on weeds that grow way too tall.
We water our hopes with laughter and light,
Sprouting new joys from the depths of the night.

With shovels of grit, we dig through the mess,
Unearthing our quirks, we often confess.
Like flowers that bloom, in the silliest hues,
We dance in the mud, wearing mismatched shoes.

So here's to the growth that comes when we stumble,
To laughter that leaves us all in a jumble.
Life's lesson is clear, when you take a big leap,
You might just find joy hidden under a heap.

Let's flourish together in this quirky parade,
Where every misstep's a new serenade.
With grit and a grin, let's take on the tide,
In our joyful garden, we'll take it all wide!

The Essence of Essence

In a cup of pure chaos, we sip with delight,
Finding humor in spills that happen at night.
Essence of sweetness, that tickles the nose,
Mixing the flavors that nobody knows.

We blend quirky fruits with a dash of strange spice,
Creating concoctions that taste more than nice.
With bubbles of giggles that rise to the top,
Our favorite creations, we never will stop.

In the kitchen of life, we're all gourmet cooks,
Stirring in laughter like good little crooks.
A recipe mutates with each brand new day,
Each drop of essence leads us astray!

So here's to the sips that make our hearts race,
In this zany old world, we find our own pace.
With a pinch of absurdity swirling around,
The essence of joy is easily found!

Fractals of Faith

In patterns of laughter, we play hide and seek,
Fractals of faith give the brave a good peek.
Round every corner, confusion does spin,
But faith's like a joke that no one can pin.

We spiral together in capsized delight,
Mirrors reflecting our flaws in plain sight.
Like a fractal of nonsense, we twirl and we twine,
Finding faith in the moments that make us divine.

The more that we stumble, the deeper we dive,
Our giggles like bubbles keep hope very alive.
With jokes as the pillars, we build with a flair,
Every quirk and mishap shows we can repair.

So dance 'round the edges of laughter and woe,
In this fractal of faith, let your mischief flow.
With lighthearted strokes, paint your world with a grin,
For the best of the journey is where we begin!

Sheltering Secrets

Beneath the wild branches, secrets abide,
Whispering tales of laughter and pride.
Sheltered in foliage, we giggle and peek,
Finding joy in the whispers, the playful and meek.

The squirrel's a spy, with eyes all aglow,
He watches our antics, enjoying the show.
In the shade of the leaves, we exchange all our quirks,
Crafting a refuge where silliness lurks.

The breeze carries giggles from tree to tree,
A band of mischief that's wild and free.
With secrets like buttons, we sew them with cheer,
Each stitch a reminder that laughter's near.

So come take a seat, under branches so wide,
Join the secret circle, let's laugh and collide.
For in this retreat, where humor is seen,
Sheltering whispers weave joy in between!

Layers of Legacy

In a forest where whispers reside,
The trees giggle as secrets collide.
Old leaves chuckle at tales of the past,
While squirrels hold treasures, their finds unsurpassed.

Bark bears the scars of stories untold,
Of acorns that dared to be brave and bold.
Branches sway lightly, gossip in the air,
While shadows dance with a silly flair.

Under the canopy, laughter unfolds,
As beetles debate who's the best at gold.
Roots intertwine like friends at a feast,
In the joyous embrace of nature's yeast.

So when you stroll through the leafy parade,
Remember the humor that's always portrayed.
For beneath all the wisdom, the laughter will soar,
In the layers of life, there's always much more.

Secrets Beneath the Bark

With each creak and groan, can you hear the jest?
The trees are experts at wearing a vest.
Their bark hides secrets, and not just the old,
But pranks that are silly and stories retold.

A squirrel once dressed in a leaf and a hat,
Declared himself king of the woodland spat.
Branches burst laughing, their roots shook with cheer,
As the wind blew a tune that everyone could hear.

In the knots of the wood, a smile takes place,
While mushrooms debate about who's got the grace.
Fungi twirl round, in a dance of delight,
Making sure fungi don't miss out on the night.

So come hear the stories that twirl in the air,
Where the whispers of trees hang loose without care.
For beneath all the bark is humor again,
In the forest of life, there's laughter with friends.

Tapestry of Time

In the weave of the woods, a fabric is spun,
A tapestry stitched with laughs, oh what fun!
Each thread tells a tale, a giggle or two,
Of critters conspiring with nothing to do.

A rabbit with sunglasses, oh what a sight!
Hops past a tree, all ready to kite.
The owls roll their eyes, wise to the trick,
While the bees buzz around, weaving in quick.

Time plays its game with shadows and light,
As branches a-sways steal the scene with delight.
A fox wears a feather; the crew is complete,
In a play of the wood, where all worlds meet.

So pause when you wander through leafy old lanes,
And catch all the giggles that echo like trains.
For the tapestry's rich with stories and cheer,
In the forest of whimsy, adventure is near.

The Core's Confession

Deep in the heart where the wild things bloom,
A secret is kept in the pitch and the gloom.
The core of the tree, with a wink and a grin,
Whispers of berries that once wore a skin.

"My friends often poke fun at my sturdy frame,
But it's all good jest, never shame in the game.
They call me a fossil, all stiff and so old,
Yet inside I'm bubbling with stories to be told.

With knots and with grooves, I carry fatigue,
While critters hold parties, their own little league.
So raise up a toast to the laughter we share,
For hidden inside is a world without care.

So when you see trees, don't pass them on by,
Listen closely and hear laughter fly high.
For the secrets they've locked all tender and sweet,
Are the echoes of joy that give rhythms their beat.

Signs on the Sapling

Look up high, a leaf's a sign,
Is it time for sun or wine?
A squirrel speaks in cheeky tone,
'This tree's a throne, you're not alone!'

The bark has jokes, it makes you laugh,
Counting rings, what a daft staff!
"If I had legs," the branch does pine,
"I'd take a stroll, might even dine!"

A shadow creeps, it has a tale,
Of foliage dreams and leaf-hungry snails.
With every rustle in the breeze,
Nature plainly teases with ease.

So gather round, my friends so dear,
The wittiest trees are always near!
They whisper secrets, soft and grand,
In this giggling grove, hand in hand.

Roots Revisited

Digging deep in playful ground,
What treasures here can be found?
The roots all giggle, do a dance,
In their old soil, they take a chance.

'Why did the apple roll away?'
A root pipes up, 'Now that's a play!
Because it saw the cider press!'
A laugh erupts, oh what a mess!

Twists and turns, a tangled spree,
"Hey look, I stumbled over me!"
Each root, a tale, a laugh, a cheer,
In this underground party, we draw near.

So come on down, join the scene,
Roots revisited, we're all keen!
With humor sprouting from the ground,
In this underworld, joy is found.

Roots of Revelation

Beneath the surface, secrets lie,
Roots gather 'round, whispering high.
"Did you hear what the twig said?"
"No, but I'm dying, let's not dread!"

The roots chuckle, a comical jest,
"Find a leaf that can take a rest!"
"Or a nut that could crack a joke,
In this realm, laughter's no smoke!"

With every tickle of tender soil,
They spin their web, they lovingly toil.
Branches quiver, what's this reveal?
A giggling trunk gives a great squeal!

It's all about roots, you see,
Digging deep sets your mind free.
So let's share laughter, revel in cheer,
In these roots, truth gives a sneer.

Chamber of Hidden Whispers

In the chamber, whispers play,
A tickling breeze in bright array.
"Did you see that nutty squirrel?"
"I hear he's off to check the whirl!"

The branches nod, they've got the scoop,
"Let's hold a party! Gather the troop!"
With acorns bouncing to the beat,
The secret songs become quite sweet.

Whispers giggle in hidden rooms,
Among the roots, ancient blooms.
"What's the best joke a tree could tell?"
"Just leaf it to me, I know it well!"

In this chamber, humor reigns,
With leaves of laughter, forget your pains.
So come inside and share the fun,
In this leafy tale, we're never done.

The Brotherhood of Bark

In the forest where secrets dwell,
Woodland critters know all too well.
A squirrel shares tales, his cheeks full of nuts,
While a wise old owl just chuckles and struts.

Rabbits wear coats, quite dapper and neat,
Debating just how to avoid a swift treat.
They giggle and chatter without any care,
In the brotherhood of bark, truth's soft as air.

Mossy old logs play tricks on the sight,
Turning shadows to pranks in the fading light.
Every tree has a story, a laugh, or a joke,
From the roots of the earth, they merrily poke.

So raise your glass made of bark and of leaf,
To friends in the wild, let's toast with belief.
For in laughter and joy, we all discover,
Life's quirky truths that will never smother.

The Hollow's Gentle Confession

In a hollow of whispers, secrets unfold,
The chipmunk recounts tales both silly and bold.
With a wink and a twitch, he spins quite the yarn,
Of tripping on acorns and costumes at dawn.

A soft tree trunk hums as it starts to confess,
About the odd raccoon who insists he's a mess.
"My stripes are quite stylish!" he declared with a grin,
As the birds burst in laughter, they chirped, "Let's begin!"

The frogs join the fun, in their croaky delight,
Creating distractions on a warm, starry night.
They make all the trees giggle so hard they turn blue,
In the hollow's embrace, they easily woo.

A squirrel quips, "What a fabulous sight!
Confessions of hollows make woodland hearts light."
With humor and charm, the forest agrees,
In sharing our quirks, we find camaraderie with ease.

Residing in Nature's Embrace

In the heart of the woods, where the air is so sweet,
Lies a band of misfits who dance on their feet.
A hedgehog in sunglasses, a fox in a hat,
Swapping tales of the day while just having a chat.

They gather each dusk under branches that sway,
With laughter and fun, they brighten the way.
Every leaf is a pillow, every path is fine,
In nature's embrace, they sip sap like wine.

The bear with a bowtie, quite dapper and spry,
Spins stories of honey that tickle the sky.
While ladybugs giggle, just flitting about,
In the circle of joy, there's never a doubt.

So come join the feast, with a smile and a grin,
Find joy in the laughter of creatures within.
In nature's embrace, each moment we trace,
Is filled with the warmth of a whimsical place.

Wisdom in the Wild's Cradle

In the cradle of wild, wisdom takes flight,
Where creatures converse in the soft evening light.
A badger once pondered, his whiskers all quirked,
"Is it me or the moon? This night's perfectly worked!"

A giraffe with big dreams peeks over the trees,
While tigers tell jokes that tickle the knees.
With laughter encircled, they share their great tales,
Of mishaps and triumphs, on land and on trails.

The bees bust a move as they hum low and sweet,
While butterflies swirl, all delicate and neat.
Old turtles roll upward, seeking the sun,
Each chuckle and giggle binds everyone.

So here's to the wisdom in laughter so bright,
In the wild's cradle of joy, it's pure delight.
Let the echoes of chuckles take root and grow wide,
For with humor and grace, we flourish with pride.

Nature's Archive of Whispers

In the woods where secrets lie,
Trees giggle as the breezes sigh.
Woodpeckers knock with playful flair,
Woodland gossip floats in the air.

Squirrels scamper, tails held high,
Plotting acorn heists, oh my!
Fungi chuckle, sprouting near,
Mushroom jokes that all can hear.

Foxes frolic, in leafy shades,
Crafting pranks in the sun's cascades.
Bees buzz loudly, making schemes,
Nature's party fuels our dreams.

Underneath the canopy wide,
All the antics that they hide.
Whispers echo, laughter's thread,
Join the fun, no need for dread!

The Grove's Silent Confidant

Amidst the thickets, secrets brew,
Old oaks gossip, sharing the view.
Branches sway with a teasing glance,
Sending leaves off for their dance.

A rabbit snickers, ears perked keen,
As squirrels share tales that are obscene.
The breeze hums tunes of playful lore,
Turned-up roots, always wanting more.

Hidden critters within the shade,
Whispered antics, a grand charade.
Laughter echoes from twig to leaf,
Nature's jesters, beyond belief!

So step on softly, join the fray,
Listen closely, come what may.
In this grove, hilarity thrives,
Nature's chuckles keep us alive.

Beneath the Crust of Existence

Digging deep in soil's embrace,
Worms wear glasses, a smart-looking face.
Roots twist & turn like old ballet,
Sharing whispers in muddy play.

Ants march in lines, quite a sight,
Singing songs of their lunch delight.
"Watch your step!" they shout with glee,
As they scatter, one, two, three!

Moles in tunnels, plotting their schemes,
Chasing echoes of distant dreams.
A dance beneath with friends so bold,
Life's jests underground, a sight to behold!

Laughter sprouts from earthy seams,
While nature sips on joyful themes.
Beneath the crust where fun persists,
Existence ticks in nature's twist!

Espousing Nature's Truths

Mountains whisper, clouds conspire,
Tales of trees that never tire.
Hedgehogs sigh with prickly pride,
As flowers bloom in colors wide.

Waves of grass sway left and right,
Tickling toes in pure delight.
Beetles boast of races won,
As petals laugh beneath the sun.

Dewdrops glisten like tiny stars,
Telling tales of falling cars!
Nature's riddle, ever so spry,
Life's a jest, oh my, oh my!

So gather round the leafy stage,
Join the revels, throw off the cage.
For nature's whimsy knows no bounds,
With every chuckle, joy abounds!

www.ingramcontent.com/pod-product-compliance
Lightning Source LLC
Chambersburg PA
CBHW051658160426
43209CB00004B/946